THE GREATER EXISTENCE

111 KEYS TO WALKING IN YOUR INFINITY

BY THE MANIFEST MENTOR

Brian Hyppolite

Copyright 2022 Naprip Publishing

All right reserved. No part of this book may be reproduced or redistributed without express consent from the author and publisher. No parts of this publication may be reproduced or transmitted in any form or by any means, mechanical or electronic, including photocopying or recording, or by any information storage and retrieval system, or transmitted by email without permission in writing from the author and publisher.

For more of the Manifest Mentor's books, classes, courses, coaching, & community please visit WWW.BRIANHYPPOLITE.COM

THIS BOOK IS DEDICATED TO MY STAFF AND FAMILY AT MANIFEST UNIVERSITY. It's a privilege to pour into you. It's an amazing honor when you pour into me. Thank you for helping me create the safest place on earth. I cherish what we share. May our cups runneth over as we grow old together. One day our grandchildren tell the story of how we defeated generational curses and created generational wealth for them as we reached for our greater existence! I love yall to life!

CONTENTS

CHAPTER 1
 The Greater 1

CHAPTER 2
 Mind control (acceptance - resistance = abundance) 28

CHAPTER 3
 Creation 46

CHAPTER 4
 Apex Belief System 63

CHAPTER 5
 Know the vibes 86

CHAPTER 6
 Walking in Your Infinity 100

CHAPTER 1

The Greater

KEY 1

Prepare to embark on your safari of life!

Welcome to a greater you, a greater existence, a greater experience, a greater expansion of life. You lack nothing. All that you need can be found within you. Nothing is missing, nothing is broken. You are filled with infinite power, capabilities, and possibilities.

KEY 2

Where your focus goes, your energy flows, and that's what grows

We will start with a breathing exercise I use in my coaching sessions to help someone get out of their head and into their soul! Where we are about to go, your mind can't lead you. This exercise requires you to place your attention on your breathing pattern and summons your focus away from the cares and worries of your day or anything your mind had anchored itself to.

Sitting still in a comfortable position, close your eyes and take 3 long breaths in and 5 short breaths out.

In between each cycle of breaths, speak - I am receptive to a higher dimension of life.

Repeat this process until it is happening without a strong amount of focus.

Making such moves takes us out of our sympathetic nervous system that wants to identify and respond to everything, and moves us into our parasympathetic state, which allows us to rest and digest.

For some, a hum also helps in the process of centering oneself. Our hum or "omm" vibrates at the frequency of 432 Hz. This is the same frequency found throughout nature and chanting it tunes your being to this frequency of universal wholeness and emphasizes a connection between you that is greater.

KEY 3

A powerful moment of meditation:

I want you to imagine yourself at the youngest age that you can remember. I want you to find your oldest favorite memory. Go as far back as you can and find the best childhood memory. Do you have it? What is it?

What did you look like? What did you love about you or your life back then?

Breath in deeply through your nose and out through your mouth; remember what smells you enjoyed and were excited by.

Take another deep breath, and as you slowly exhale, roll your tongue across the roof of your mouth and remember what tastes your tastebuds couldn't wait to taste!

Remember if it was cold or hot, sunny, raining or windy. Breath in deeply through your nose and out through your mouth; repeat breathing slowly.

Now, I want you to imagine your most powerful and abundantly amazing life. How would your life look if the universe handed you a blank check and you could have what you've always wanted with no limits? What does that experience look like? Where do you live, what do you wear, what kind of love is in your life, what do you do for a living, who are you serving, who is serving you, who is with you? Breath in deeply through your nose and out through your mouth slowly.

Both images represent realities that are available to you. The vision of your past and the vision of your future both represent 2 realities that are compatible with your existence and sit in your possibilities of alignment. Believe in them both.

KEY 4

Acknowledge you have come to this place, this moment, this intersection of time and space for a divine opportunity to reach a greater level of existence.

We want to tap into our divinity or divine energy to best participate in this divine opportunity. My first book, MANIFESTING YOU: 111 KEYS TO UNLOCKING YOUR DIVINITY, is a great place to start if what I'm saying is already going over your head. As the great James Baldwin once said, "If I speak above your head, then I'm speaking where your head should be."

We all have what I call a "godstate". Before you can access it, you must identify with the god within you. You have become used to identifying yourself by where you are from and what you've been through. No one ever told you to identify yourself by what's within you.

If you do not acknowledge that greater is available to you, you will avoid greatness.

KEY 5

Get on your level

An honest period of self-assessment is required. Use this page to answer this question and put a date next to it. We will come back here for another honest assessment later in our safari.

Where are you at in these areas on a scale of 1-10? (1 is not good, 10 being greatest)

- ○ Self-identification
- ○ Self-love
- ○ Self-respect
- ○ Self-discipline
- ○ Self-healing
- ○ Self-awareness

KEY 6

Repeat these affirmations

I love all that is coming before me

I am an extension of source energy

I see endless opportunities, and I will enjoy aligning with the one that aligns with me

I am elated to be in the place of alignment and opportunity

I like the forward motion feeling I am feeling

I am seeing universal energy responding to my thoughts

I enjoy the assurance and confirmations I receive that I am in alignment with divine energy and operating on frequencies of abundance

I feel empowered and highly capable

I love that I am my greatest source of solutions and not my biggest source of problems

I am at peace and experiences thoughts of pleasure and abundance

I am happy that I am attracting aligned relationships that increase all that is positive within me

I enjoy seeing all that is great within me influence greatness on other people and other environments

I love this power I possess to be greater than I have ever been

I welcome my glory. I welcome an outpouring of God's abundance

I can feel the presence of God in all that I do

I love the feeling of clarity and understanding that is within me

I am grateful for all of my experiences, and I can see how they have prepared me to excel at this very moment

I love that I have released lack, accepted abundance, and begun walking in my infinity.

KEY 7

If you can tell me how you have been hurt, I can point you in the direction of who you are supposed to help. Your human side is for who the god in you connects to. Take a moment to answer these questions.

What change do you want to see in the world?

_____
_____
_____
_____

Who are you sent to heal?

_____
_____
_____
_____
_____
_____

Is there anything that touches you so deeply that it drives you? Often, a powerful purpose can come from powerful pain.

_____
_____
_____
_____
_____
_____

KEY 8

Identify your godstate.

There are 4 dimensions and components of your existence. You are comprised of mind, body, spirit, and energy. Regardless of religion or spiritual preference, we all agree that the spirit or soul is connected to the great source, divine creator, holy spirit, or whatever almighty energy you subscribe to. Suppose it's the soul that has an active relationship and path of communication with whatever you acknowledge to be of greater and higher power. In that case, you must learn to identify with that part of you the most. You must also learn to yield all other components of your being to the will of your soul so your soul can lead you to that greater power within and teach you how to use it. Spirituality means to know something beyond the physical.

KEY 9

Tap into your godstate.

What I call the godstate is simply existing in the high vibration of who and what you truly are; the likeness of God. Your godstate is the existence you experience when your soul is at the wheel of your life, providing direction and guidance. Your mind is only useful for reference in navigating your life. It may help in navigation by offering logistics and references, but your mind should never be left in charge to choose the destination. Your soul is the component of your existence, and it is best fit for this important decision.

If you see yourself from your godstate, you will make decisions and movements from your godstate; you will access the power of your godstate and begin to walk in your infinity. We are all a part of a great spirit we refer to as god, and because you are a part of God, you are god.

KEY 10

A life ruled by the 5 senses is a life of great limitations.

They are only good for survival. All senses are tied to perception, and sensory perception is limited. If I show you my hand, you can only see one side at a time. Try as you might, with all of the sightseeing skills in the world; there will always be another side of my hand that you cannot see.

In order to truly live, you must move out of a life navigated by your sensory perception and start a life directed by your inner perception. The ways of survival will always be tied to a place of lack and limitation.

KEY 11

What is manifesting?

Manifesting is the act of turning a thought into a thing. It is the ritual of taking something out of your mind and placing it in your possession using your energy and intention. What do you want to manifest? Use this space to write it down.

KEY 12

What is your INFINITY?

Your infinity is the limitless abundance of all that is great and divine within you. Walking in your infinity yields results that you know you alone can't take credit for. The term "blessings there aren't room enough to receive" comes to mind. I'm talking about overflow, more than enough, can't hide this because it's too big not to be seen as a kind of abundance. Your infinity is renewable and sustainable, just like EVERYTHING ELSE CREATED BY GOD ENERGY! Anything that is rooted in lack is an outright opposing enemy of abundance and the way of all that is related to God.

KEY 13

Learn & apply the universal laws

You are vibration. Asssuming we took away everything we dress ourselves up in and as if we are stripped away of every fabric or any fabric of identity, how would you be identified? By your vibration. Vibration is energy, and all energy observes certain rules or laws. As a being of energy, if you do not obtain the proper knowledge and utilization to have the laws of energy working for you, they will forever be of detrimental occurrence to you, naturally working against you. Turning the understandings into overstanding will bring many benefits.

There are atleast 88 universal laws that effect our daily realities. This universe sits perfectly balanced on an axel of perfect, natural, and moral laws that maintain order and harmony. When you exist in harmony with these laws, you can be assured of an eventual positive outcome. You can be assured of suffering when you exist outside of these laws. The purpose of that suffering is to indicate to you that there is a better choice to make, another path to take that will not lead to suffering.

Look these up for yourself. Their originals far exceed any European scholar you may find speaking on it. This is ancient wisdom and stolen knowledge, so wherever you find it, TAKE IT BACK!

I have listed a few of the Universal laws I see working all around me that people around me clearly don't see. Next to each law, I have written the interpretation of its meaning.

KEY 14

THE LAW OF ATTRACTION

Although most are commonly aware of this law, they don't understand it or use it for a greater existence. Instead, they attract things to them that they'd rather not have. The law of attraction doesn't respond to what you want or what you ask for; it responds to what you feel and what you are. Again, you are vibration/energy. This law brings you other energies that match the vibration you offered it.

KEY 15

THE LAW OF MANIFESTING

Everything begins with a thought or idea. Ideas and experiences form beliefs and habits. To change a reality, you must first change the way of your belief. Beliefs can be changed when you acknowledge a current belief system and behavior pattern is not working for you and apply a new set of beliefs and supportive behaviors. Eliminate all ideas, vibrations, and actions that are disharmonious to what you desire for your reality. Apply focus, effort, and energy to all that feed and nurture the ideas, vibrations, and actions of the reality you desire.

KEY 16

THE LAW OF CONSCIOUS DETACHMENT

A master of life accepts all that is good allows all that is negative from life to flow through him, never becoming attached to him. It is your resistance to what is that offers you suffering. Suffering comes from sadness. A lack of acceptance will create sadness. As each day passes and the sadness compounds, you are removed further and further away from the vibrational reality you belong in. Suffering with no end in sight leads to a low frequency we identify as depression. If we are unable to release the feelings and happenings we experience throughout life, they will rot in us in a way that would allow scar tissue to feel like an open wound.

KEY 17

THE LAW OF FELLOWSHIP

This law observes the amazing and unmistakable power of compounded and multiplied faith. Whether it's two or more gathered in the same room or intentions linked to a desire and tied to a combined belief, there is undeniable power when hearts, minds, and spirits direct their focus on the same thing.

KEY 18

THE LAW OF RESISTANCE

That which You resist draws to you. You will encounter it until you learn to deal with it. You will retake the test until you pass it! You will continue to be prepared for it by being forced to deal with it, until you DEAL WITH IT!

KEY 19

THE LAW OF SELF WORTH

You will only attract what you believe you deserve.

KEY 20

Change how you approach the universe/god/ancestor/greater power

When you are constantly asking the universe to give to you, and have been repetitively chanting phrases like "give me this, give me that! I want this, I want that! I need and give me more", it's not uncommon for the universe to respond accordingly and then saying "give me this, and give me that, give give give give". Now you can't receive because you find yourself in a perpetual state of having to give because the universe is doing to you exactly what you are doing to it.

... now if you approach the universe with "how may I serve you", the universe responds with an energy of serving you as well.

KEY 21

Are you serving your ego or your purpose?

What is a server? A server brings you requested items that match what you articulated you desired and/or required. Are you bringing about what your ego has articulated it desired? Or what your purpose has articulated it required. You are god and have a god energy. At every instance and at all times, you have a choice and chance to either BUILD or DESTROY with the power of your energy and intention. No man can serve two masters.

My brothergod from Manifest University, Al Tutson, once said, "ego stands for Edging God Out!"

KEY 22

You are not a human being struggling to have a spiritual experience; you are a spiritual being struggling with your human experience.

You are here for a divine reason that far exceeds you. If you're hearing this, you are an amazing soul; everything is going to be just fine. This is your truth. Truth is not something you have to agree with; it's something you yield to. I'm speaking to the part of you which knows this already. To change your thinking, you need to change who you believe you are.

KEY 23

Level up

A person living a level 2 life and using a level 2 mindset can handle level 1 problems easily and have yet to master level 2 problems. This person is due to be overwhelmed and most likely trumped by a level 5 problem. That same level 5 problem is lightweight to a level 8 person using their level 8 mindset. A level 10 person dealing with a level 10 problem isn't dealing with a problem at all; they are just dealing with what must be dealt with at that level.

KEY 24

Grow yourself to be bigger than your problems.

If you are smart, you know how to handle your vital assets. You can grow yourself, intellect, mentality, and abilities to match, rival, and conquer the opposition you face at each level of life. You can use the wisdom gained from successes and failures on each previous level; you help you be more efficient and effective at your current one.

KEY 25

What is alignment?

Alignment is harmony being obtained by all 4 dimensions of your existence; mind, body, spirit, and energy. This is when all of the above mentioned is working collectively and in unison towards the obtainment of a goal or vibrational existence. Creating an environment of alignment within you at all costs must be a priority to you.

This reminds me of THE UNIVERSAL LAW OF CORRESPONDENCE. This law states that harmony can always be found and obtained between the great physical plane, the great mental plane, and the great spiritual plane. This is great news since you exist simultaneously in all these and all dimensions! The law further reveals that not only can each plane of existence operate in harmony, but every individual thing in each plane can work in harmony and towards your benefit.

CHAPTER 2

Mind control
(acceptance - resistance = abundance)

KEY 26

Take control of your reality

Have you taken control of your life, or still living by accident? If living by accident, anxiety and stress is normal. Control does not have anxiety or stress. Acceptance does not have anxiety or stress. Begin to take control of your life by being utterly responsible for it. The quickest way to have power is to exercise intentions. The fastest way to lose power is to not move with intentions.

KEY 27

Your mental and emotional stages will either grow or go in cycles.

Your emotions do not create; emotions are merely indicators of what you are creating. All other creatures only suffer from creation. Humans are the only ones who suffer from what they created (in their minds). Many suffer from being on this spiritual journey using mental and emotional navigation. Have a mind that is open to everything and attached to nothing. Have an open mind; a closed mind doesn't get fed either.

KEY 28

Negative emotions are an indication that you are viewing something from a place separate from your divinity/source energy.

Your circumstances have very little to do with what you experience in life. It's your perspective that creates this.

There is also understanding, grace, mercy, compassion, and empathy for others in your divinity. Pressure, stress, and suffering are to be expected when you have not figured out how to conduct your mind and emotions.

KEY 29

Pick a direction and build momentum

Your mind predominately focuses on one thing at a time. Every minute, the focus of your life keeps shifting. So, your life and energy do not know where to go. Life only looks complicated when it lacks direction. Life is not complicated. The systems you added to your life have become complicated, but life is still simple. Life is happening effortlessly in seasons without missing a beat. If you are in this time and space to direct your thought and energy in such a way that the momentum of those thoughts and that energy cannot be stopped by any opposing force.

The walls you build as self-protection also become the walls of self-imprisonment.

KEY 30

Memory is a cocoon of the past. In it, there is safety, but also imprisonment.

The memory is that which does not exist but acts out as if it does. Since your memory cannot create, it will manipulate your emotions to create a new experience for you.

Memory realigns us with the feeling and vibration of that old thing. Memory is an old conversation that wants to be had again.

KEY 31

EVERY SUBJECT IS TWO SUBJECTS: What is wanted and the absence of it.

Most people think they are thinking about getting money, when really what they are meditating on is their lack of it and the problems that could cause. Sometimes you may intend to be thinking about improving a relationship, but if we examined your thoughts and words, they represented the problems or faults of your partner or a particular situation you are unpleased with. You are, in fact, focusing on the negative instead of the positive experience that you desire.

Do you see how if you aren't intentional with your mind, how it can easily play this trick on you?

KEY 32

If you don't take control of your mind, it will control you.

You will come to understand the power of your mind in one of two ways.

1. You will create the life you desire and realize you pulled generational wealth and abundance out of your genius brain, and you can continue to manifest your thoughts into things through your infinite source.

2. Your mind becomes so far gone that its now a mountain so high that you can't see beyond it and won't even dare climb it.

KEY 33

Your mind is a garden that you must tend to daily.

Conversations and thoughts often leave debris in the field of our minds that must be cleared, and weeds must be uprooted. Unfruitful seeds of thought that are given a chance to take root in your mind will act as weeds and begin to choke out what is good and healthy.

After you work in your garden, relax and enjoy the growth, chill out, be nicer to yourself, think more thoughts about yourself (and others) that feel good. Don't work so hard. give yourself a break. Do more of the things that make you happy.

KEY 34

You aren't suffering from the event; you are suffering from the meaning you've attached to it.

If you don't change the meaning associated with your feelings, emotions, and the things you experience, you will continue to suffer from them. In addition, you won't be able to guide your thoughts at the early, minuscule, and subtle stages. If you can't guide your thoughts at their early, minuscule, and subtle stages, you won't be able to control them; you start to get more thoughts that support them, or when the law of attraction kicks in and compounds those thoughts with greater and greater momentum.

Pain is inevitable; suffering is optional.

KEY 35

YOU CANNOT DEMAND YOURSELF INTO ALIGNMENT. YOU CANNOT WORK YOURSELF INTO ALIGNMENT. YOU CANNOT EFFORT YOURSELF INTO ALIGNMENT.

You've got to release and let go of everything that offers resistance to your alignment. Everything you want already is! If you pay attention to how you feel, release the things you shouldn't keep, release the resistance, you will step right into the path of abundance. You cannot create outside of your vibrational offering and reality. You can't overcompensate with actions to make up for incorrect energy.

KEY 36

If you stop using your memory to guide you, the past cannot recycle itself through you.

You were born to direct your thoughts, not be directed by them. You are meant to use your emotions, not be controlled by them. Making movements based on the past may easily damage the present and cripple future possibilities. Stay connected to source, self, and soul. Allow them to guide you. Cycles stop when you do something new! You cannot be moving in the power of your intentions if you are reacting to something in your present based on what happened in your past.

KEY 37

Learn to respond and not react.

A response is connected to your preset agenda and acknowledged alignment. A reaction is often unthought of and thought out.

A response is the action required to further the agenda or alignment despite an adverse or unpleasant situation. A reaction is knee-jerk behavior in correspondence to an adverse or unpleasant situation.

A response is connected to the long-term goal. A reaction is connected to the moment of adversity.

A response moves with opportunity. A reaction moves from the opposition.

KEY 38

If you are unhappy, especially for a long period of time, you have been practicing the vibration of the problem.

You have been practicing the vibration of the problem so intensely that you are oblivious, blind to, and most importantly, out of touch with the solution. You have been identifying with the weight of a problem, not your strength and ability to solve it. You have been thinking thoughts that don't make you feel good and dwelling on them long enough to sink to their vibration. Progress is impossible if you always do things the way you've done things.

We experience what is commonly identified as being overwhelmed when our solutions are outnumbered by our problems. Pay attention to your vibrational reality. Most people are offering much of their energy/vibration to what they are observing, not what they wish to create, so they end up creating on the vibration they are observing. This world teaches you to do all external management but does not teach you internal management.

KEY 39

Ask yourself: How much attention to a problem is a beneficial amount?

You cannot see a solution while starring at a problem. If you stop focusing on what isn't working and direct your attention, energy, and vibration to what is working and the things you do like, you are more likely to reach the clarity you need to solve the problem you had. Physically, you are made up of 90% water, and water boils when it is overwhelmed with heat. The same way you cant see to the bottom of a boiling pot of water, you cannot see clearly to make proper judgements when overwhelmed with thought or emotion (both of which you created, by the way)

Take a step back. When you come out of a state of resistance, you come into a state of receptance.

KEY 40

Schedule your thoughts like you schedule your day.

Write out what you need to be thinking about throughout your day. I've seen some people create a general list of what they need to focus on each day in order to keep their mind where it needs to be. My approach is more like or a detailed calendar that reflects what you need to be thinking about on an hourly basis.

KEY 41

It's time to think about what you think about.

It also may be a good idea to chart out what you think about during the day just to get some true data & analytics of where your mind spends its time.

This will especially help if you have been having trouble focusing. You must become highly intentional to direct your focus! If you don't stay focused long enough to get momentum, you will not build up strength and endurance to make it past the distractions, let alone any opposing force.

KEY 42

Speak these affirmations over your life and legacy

This is a great day! I am connected to abundance because I am connected to the source energy within me.

My authenticity brings me power, and I use that power to prosper in my purpose.

Everything is working out for me. I have released all resistance to my abundance.

I have laid down every mindset, action, reaction, behavior, and energy that creates a resistance to my peace, power, prosperity and joy!

Today I will not create limitations.

Today will be a day well-lived.

On this great day, I will remain open to the pleasure life has to offer me and is here to bring me.

Today I will get closer to my goals. Today I will avoid the distractions of anything not related to my purpose or goals.

I will move in alignment with the vibration of my greatest self.

I accept that I am exactly where I am supposed to be right now, and there is something that will add to my ability to have peace, power, prosperity, and joy.

CHAPTER 3

Creation

KEY 43

The only way for your will to be done in the NOW is for you to be creating and creating ways for it to prosper.

You are either creating a reality or calibrating to a reality. If you aren't calibrating to coexist with something, you are manipulating it to coexist with it. Manipulation is a form of creating the reality you desire.

KEY 44

You are an alchemist.

You have the gift of alchemy. Alchemy is the ability to transmute, transform, and transport energy. Alchemy is your power to manipulate and influence energy.

Undoubtedly, you have been face to face with an energy you did not like or welcome before. Think of a time when you used your influence, energy and intention to reject and redirect the energy that was not desired energy in order to create the environment that was. If you have stopped a fight or been the cooler head that prevailed, you have used alchemy. Get more familiar with your power.

KEY 45

Creating the reality you desire means not aligning with any energy or frequency that is not intuned or working in harmony with what I desire.

A major misunderstanding I get to unravel for many people in my coaching sessions is that creating the reality you desire isn't about building a whole new world; it's largely about removing and rejecting the things you don't want. In the presence of peace, you will naturally create, cultivate, attract and sustain all that is for you.

KEY 46

Begin to use your creativity like never before.

What have you been yearning to create or have a desire to learn how to create? Explore and explode with creativity.

KEY 47

Life is a menu. You may choose something different.

I recommend ordering something related to your purpose. Create around your purpose. Plan around your purpose. A plan is an exaggeration of today. It's good to have a plan, but it's more important to have a purpose. When plans fall apart, purpose will remain.

KEY 48

Create new habits that support your alignment.

Old habits die hard, but new habits come on strong. Old habits only seem to die hard because of the excuses we use to hold onto these old habits. We still enjoy the benefit of the old habit; whether it's a result or a familiarity, as long as we enjoy the benefit, we will make excuses to keep experiencing it. New habits come on strong because they are often accompanied by excitement, new challenges, and things that have no problem pulling you back.

KEY 49

Never become so in love with the creation that you forget about the creator.

This goes for anything you create: a vibrational reality, a mental reality, a physical reality, or a spiritual reality. This is also applicable when/if you become so wrapped up in yourself that you disregard you are also a creation, forgetting about the creator.

KEY 50

Create out of your sustainable abundance.

We have discussed how you are godly, godlike, god energy, and so on. The god within you has entered this time and space in this human form to pull from the human experience and create a divine reality with your god power. You are not here for yourself; you have a divine mission. You are to create and complete work, evolution, and ascension.

KEY 51

Create an environment that brings your vision to life.

How are you consciously creating your space?

KEY 52

Create a purpose product or a servant's service.

If you put your pain, passion, and purpose together, you will create something that helps others. Tell your story so that when others hear it, it will help them. When you hear it, it will help you.

KEY 53

What Are Your Intrinsic Strengths?

Take the time to analyze and make a list of where your natural talents are. Are you an analytical thinker who excels at strategizing? Are you a detail-oriented person who has always been great at noticing what other people look over? Are you the neighborhood "connector" who's great at bringing people together? Are you a "kid at heart" who can be silly and fun with your younger family members?

KEY 54

What are the activities that make you smile, laugh, and feel most fulfilled?

Make a list of activities you may have enjoyed when you were younger. When we were younger, we were less jaded from school, work, and outside opinions: we liked what we liked. Try to tap into that younger version of yourself. It's likely she'll remind you of what you used to love, and you can find that again.

KEY 55

What motivates you?

There are two types of motivation: intrinsic and extrinsic. The former is the motivation that's found within —it's that "something" inside of you that drives you and your actions. Extrinsic motivation is the kind of motivation that we find outside of ourselves. It might be a monetary reward or an accolade of some kind. Identify what motivates you in both categories.

KEY 56

Life is an infinite number of doorways.

If you are very diligent, you will open a few of them. If you are brilliant, you will open many of them, but they will open for you if you are truly vibrant. Do not commit to a certain concept of success or a particular path of success. Have a plan but don't commit to it either. Commit to evolving your plans as you evolve to match your divine purpose and corresponding goals.

KEY 57

Make a contract with the universe.

This is an agreement regarding an exchange of energy. Write down and read aloud. Your contract should include the following:

- what you are going to do. (The labor or service you intend to provide)

- who your labor or service is going to help

- how much you intend/demand to be compensated for your labor or service.

- the time frame of which this labor and services will be completed

- what you are going to do with my profit to further add value or benefit the universe. (how will your being blessed help others?)

You are such a god that God will allow you to get and do what you say.

KEY 58

Speak these affirmations over your life!

I find comfort in knowing the divine power within me knows the path I should take that will have the least resistance and offer the most joy. Today I will live out my purpose. I know, and I understand that I have entered this space of reality at this time for a purpose greater than I.

Today, I will direct my thoughts and intentions in the direction of my purpose.
I am aware that if I respond to things differently, I can get different things out of them. Today, I will not relinquish my control over how I respond to the events of life.

What happens throughout my day will not dictate my attitude, outlook, or how I feel.

I have already made it up in my mind that peace and clarity and purpose rule and reign in my life.

I will only direct my energy towards what will bring an abundance of the things I want to be present in my life.

I am connected to my highest vibration.

I am connected to the infinite possibilities of peace, power, prosperity, and joy!

CHAPTER 4

Apex Belief System

KEY 59

DO YOU KNOW THE TRUTH OF YOUR EXISTENCE? Or are you only familiar with how you've been trained to exist?

Are you identifying yourself with things that are not you? We often do this to create a sense of self. This practice moves you from untruth to untruth. It is important to know yourself and operate in the truth of who you are, not who you have been conditioned to be, not who people want or expect you to be, and not even who you are used to being.

KEY 60

Live in a state of non-identification and liberation cannot be denied to you.

Your identity is your first limitation. Whatever you identify as, your ego sets out to protect. As I stated in the previous chapter on the power of your mind, mental barriers formed as protection also serve as a cage. This cage is the home of limited beliefs and actions. Your pride safeguards a faithful environment for your identity to frolic. Your intellect will provide whatever is needed to sustain your identity. Knowledge and evidence that corresponds with your identity are judged, shunned, and disregarded.

KEY 61

Reject weak identities and fragile spirits

It seems identities require bodyguards. Most urges for protection stem from an idea or feeling of a lack of security, so why aren't identities safe? Because they aren't the truth, and anything that isn't the truth is constantly threatened by truth. Your identity is so fragile that I don't even need to attack you to affect you; all I have to do is attack someone who identifies the same as you, and you will be provoked to react.

KEY 62

You are not uniquely defective.

Release the idea that your life experience has rendered you unusable, unrelatable and/or unreachable. Accept that your uniqueness and authenticity that makes you valuable.

KEY 63

Begin to recognize your infinity.

The people who take the limits off their lives accomplish the most and seem to have the most fun while doing it. No limit people have adapted no limit mindsets. They don't see limits. They see infinite possibilities. No limit people take what they are, accept it, and don't tell themselves they are deficient due to something they believe they lack.

KEY 64

Locate the happiness within and sit there.

You were taught to be happy with what you have, but you must start by being happy with yourself. You were taught to do the things that make you happy, but you must be the thing that makes you happy. You were taught to be with the people who make you happy, but you must be that person first.

KEY 65

The company you keep

If I leave you alone in a room all by yourself and you're capable of being miserable, that means you are in bad company and have to fix that. Take time to take inventory of your being and confront whatever stands in the way of your inner peace and appreciation.

KEY 66

Self-healing does not take time.

Self-healing occurs the moment you arrive at acceptance of what was and what is. Self-healing happens the moment you acknowledge that the cause of the pain has expired, and you release whatever anchored you to the memory and vibration of pain. What takes time is the opportunity to live and work out your healing in your life's actions. The chance to exercise your healed parts take time. But that is not to be confused with the actual healing process.

KEY 67

Don't complicate things

Wisdom loves simplicity. A chess game can be won in 5 moves. Combat can be over in 5 moves. A major goal can be accomplished in 5 moves. Focus on your needly movers. Everything else should be deleted, delegated, or delayed.

If we aren't doing the things that matter most, we won't move forward the way we should.

KEY 68

Stick to successful systems

A system = consistently following a designated process. Reinventing wheels will keep you at a low performance/amateur level. Don't start with "easy"; start with what matters. Develop momentum around what matters. You become the greatest by the practice of certain practices.

KEY 69

You manage what you measure.

Self-evaluation is imperative and is the difference between a low performance and a high performance person. Daily asking questions to get to better performance is the key to a better performance.

KEY 70

If it's not on your calendar, it is a dead dream.

Your success and each element of it must be scheduled in your life. People at the highest level of success are all strategic, prepared, & disciplined. Low performance people have goals, but they are an interest, not a commitment. It's a hope, not a demand. There's a difference between entanglement and devotion. We get entangled when we are attached to the outcome.

KEY 71

Identify with your limitless possibilities

You are a high performer, now prove it.

You are a way maker, now make it.

You are divine god energy, now be it.

KEY 72

Your next/higher level requires your next/higher level of thinking and execution.

Good people fail to become great people because common sense is not common practice. Most people don't make it to the next level because they ignore the advice FROM PEOPLE AT THE NEXT LEVEL.

KEY 73

Childhood may shape us, but it doesn't have to control us.

We can collapse a lot of time that is normally dedicated to the idea that childhood traumas and wounds have to have control over how you experience your life. Again, these events may shape us, but they do not have to control us. Triggers reveal what still needs to be healed. Release the thought that triggers, do not force yourself to respond in a certain way and become fully responsible for what you do at all times.

KEY 74

Don't ask for help if you are going to stay in a place where help won't go.

The universe/god/ancestor/higher power sends all the help that is needed to create worlds, but if you sit in a low vibrational reality, practicing the vibration of your problems, you will not be compatible, aligned, or on the same frequency as what you asked for.

KEY 75

Let go of your villains.

If you still have villains, you still see yourself as a victim. If you want to leave victimhood behind, you must release the need to tell a victimized story that has bad guys in it.

KEY 76

Let's turn you into a pyramid!

The bottom of your pyramid is made of early life experiences. The next level up is knowledge and understandings. The level above that represents overstanding and habits. The next level is your identities and excuses. The top-level is your truth and godstate.. We want to view and execute from the top of our pyramid as much as possible. If you become aware that you are moving and thinking from a lower level, please reevaluate what is controlling your focus and energy.

KEY 77

Become an apex thinker!

See everything from the apex point of your pyramid. Apex thinking is a term I created that references one's ability to identify, align, and move from their apex of thought and reasoning and not the lower levels of their existence.

KEY 78

Keep your purpose positioned at the top of your pyramid.

Every other section of your pyramid will lead to a lack of clarity. The feeling of a lack of clarity leads to the feeling of lack of direction. A lack of direction leads to a lack of action. That lack of action leads to a lack of decision-making. This all started with a lack of clarity or certainty that deals with your ego, not your purpose.

KEY 79

Alter your mindset.

Wealthy people live in a world of abundance. Poor people live in a world of limitations.

Poor people think there's not enough to go around in the world. They come from a fear-based mindset. Their answers are "either/or," but never "both." In a poor person's mindset, they go for security above love, safety before self-expression, and protection over possibility.

Wealthy people understand that with a little creativity, a willingness to be unconventional, and an open mind, they can have both. When you build your life on the "Both" mentality, you will see opportunities that you were once blind to.

Are you a possibility theorist or a fear-based thinker?

KEY 80

Speak these affirmations over yourself aloud and repetitively

I am safe and secure.

I am rooted in this present moment.

My body is my home, and I pledge to always build it up and never tear it down.

My body is a safe home for my radiant spirit.

I vibrate powerful, abundant, peaceful energy and attract this same energy in return.

Deep inner peace is my natural state.

I cultivate an atmosphere that promotes freedom of ideas.

If I am ever unsure, stillness brings the truth of myself back to me.

I am grateful to know that I am always deeply loved and supported by this Universe.

I deeply appreciate my ability to remain calm and peaceful in all situations.

I am grateful for the abundance of strength that radiates throughout my entire body.

I build my life on the foundation of faith, peace, love, purpose, and alignment.

I am whole and complete, exactly as I am.

I trust that my life is what it needs to be

I release and abandon every thought and path that offers resistance to my abundance

CHAPTER 5

Know the vibes

KEY 81

Your vibration is currency.

You have a vibrational reality that you have been completely ignoring. It's like having an inheritance sitting in a bank account, and you never access the funds or what the funds may grant you access to all because you have never used this particular bank before. Sounds insane, right? You have ignored your vibrational reality because you are so caught up in your physical, mental, emotional, and psychological realities.

If you don't figure out how to become a greater vibrational match to what you are and what is, you will stay being a vibrational match to what was.

KEY 82

Do you want to be in control of your vibration? Do you believe you have control over your vibration? Are you struggling with controlling your vibration?

One thing that helps is to look back and reflect on some of your manifestations. Pull from the glory of what you've already accomplished when it comes to taking something out of your mind and putting it into your hands. Gratitude and appreciation raise your vibration and fix your energy on your ability to receive. You will remind yourself that you have to relax, align, and allow what you need to come to you just as in the past.

KEY 83

Get quiet. You can't hear the answer if you're talking.

Take a deep breath, inhale, accepting all that is great and peaceful, and exhale releasing all that is negative. Calm your mind; your thoughts are too tense. You must massage your thoughts into a better space of calmness because you won't do anything the way you need to do it in a state of calamity. That is really what it's all about. That is really the work that you must do. I understand it will feel unnatural and counter-intuitive because your human mind is used to relying on actions to make things happen. But if you have ever stepped into alignment before, you know YOUR ACTION IS MINUSCULE IN COMPARISON WITH THE POWER & LEVERAGE OF A PROPER VIBRATIONAL REALITY AND ALIGNMENT WITH YOUR DIVINITY

KEY 84

You cannot outperform unalignment and low vibrations.

People get stuck in traps and ruts and lack because they attempt to offer hard work and choreographed behavior to compensate for their lack of alignment and not using their energy in a productive way. When life doesn't line up and go the way they desire, they get caught up in what is not happening for them, thoughts of lack and not enough coincide with the thoughts of what's not working. It's natural to want to even the odds out with hard work. What follows is usually longer hours of forced tasks under mental pressure and scrutiny, ending in a crash of a now overly tired, discouraged, doubtful energy and lowered vibration.

KEY 85

Turn on your ability to receive.

In order to receive, you must be tuned in. You are probably working too hard with your mind and not enough with your soul and vibrational reality. Your mind is tired because it was never meant to lift the weight of what your spirit carries. If we paid attention to our vibrational reality, we'd notice we have shut off our ability to receive as we focused so much on creating with the work of our hands.

KEY 86

Tune into with the right frequency.

Think of yourself as a radio for a moment. If you want to receive what 98.7fm has to offer, you must tune into that frequency. You must get onto that frequency; that's the only way it's going to work. That's the only way you will be receptive, get reception, and receive from that channel. And guess what, if you're not tuned in, you will miss the broadcast every time. Tuning into abundance and the high vibrations you need to exist in is the same way.

I need you to know that your divinity is the broadcasting tower that is transmitting everything you need, all that you are, and all that is attached to your divine purpose. If you can accept this truth, then you can tune yourself to the high vibration, and everything will flow.

KEY 87

Harness the power of your vibration by directing your energy and intention.

You could have 5 important things in your life, and 4 of them are going extremely well, and 1 of them isn't doing so well. We tend to believe we need to "go fix" the one that isn't doing well. As you do, you again try to overcompensate with actions and work to make it better. This takes you out of tune and disconnects you from that high frequency and place of reception that was working well for you. You have redirected your focus to the problem and attached your energy to the frequency of the problem.

The frequency of the problem isn't yours, so when you align yourself with it, you will begin to get unhappy and feel drained. You have taken your focus and energy off the 4 that were working well. Now, you barely have energy for the 4 that are working well, and ultimately, more things will stop working for you too.

Now, in reverse, you could have 1 thing going great and 4 things going horribly. Suppose you were to focus on the 1 thing that is going great and remained in the alignment that was allowing you to prosper. In that case, the other 4 things will eventually sort themselves out, or you will eventually receive the clarity you needed to handle them properly. YOU MUST STAY CONNECTED TO THE RECEIVING MODE!

KEY 88

Get in receiving mode

When you feel you must work hard to manufacture the reality you desire, you are working in resistance to the great force within you that is capable of bringing things to you. All of your labor is contrary to what your inner being knows. If your mind and soul aren't operating together, your heart and body don't know what to do. Your wires feel crossed. You're burning out. You are exhausting your mind and body; meanwhile, your soul is aware of its readiness and willingness to work for you and with you, but you have to allow it to work sometimes. YOU HAVE TO BE IN RECEIVING MODE!

KEY 89

Love and appreciation are the same vibrations

Suppose you are staying in the space of gratitude and gratefulness, counting your blessings, looking at all of the positives in your life, doing the things that make you feel good and thinking the thoughts that make you feel happy. In that case, you are keeping your receiving mode active and out of a reactionary state.

KEY 90

The receiving mode is also the replenishing mode.

This is where you will get stamina, clarity, vitality, and good ideas. But when we look around, we see most people react to the things they don't like rather than identifying what they want and sticking with it regardless of what challenges may come.

Reacting to what you don't want is a fast way to lose what you desire. What you are actually doing is directing your concentration, focus, and energy to the problem. You began to practice/operate on a vibration that is contrary to what you want. You are now out of harmony with what you want.

KEY 91

There are no justified resentments.

Resentments chain the weights of mental and emotional burdens to you that hold you down and slow you down. Resentments will create a state of disparity that ties you to a place of lack and removes you from the place of abundance... you must send blame out of your life and take full responsibility. Giving someone your blame also gives them your power. You may need to go pick up and reclaim some power you have left behind at a few places. Victimizing and self-sabotaging are like stray cats that run in packs. If you feed one, the other eventually shows up looking for a meal too.

KEY 92

Be intentional to focus on the vibration of the truth of your existence.

When people tell me they can't attract abundance or always attract the wrong kind of people.... Did it ever occur to you that you are sending that very same message into the universe? Is this energy the truth of who and what you are, or is this a frequency that you have become used to practicing?

Suppose you have the power to cause inner sadness and depression, which is compounded and concentrated negative emotion aimed in one direction. In that case, you also have the ability to cause inner happiness and peace with compounded and concentrated positive emotion aimed in one direction.

KEY 93

Speak these affirmations over you and your life

I have everything I need.

I nurture my body with what it needs to flourish.

I am respecting my body's need to rest and my mind's need to recharge.

I am grateful for the current opportunity to reach my goals and highest potential.

I love this feeling of high vibration

It is natural for me to experience love and joy.

My life moves in harmony and ease.

I will conduct my mind and emotions in a way that does not lead to stress or anxiety.

I enjoy identifying my plan, creating my plan, and executing my plan

I rely on my inner knowing and intuition to guide me.

I am fully present in this moment of gratitude.

I am aware of the boundless amount of wonderful things that await me.

CHAPTER 6

Walking in Your Infinity

KEY 94

When Do You Find Yourself in "Flow?

A "flow state" is when you're so deeply absorbed in an activity you kind of "lose yourself" in it. Psychology calls it "a cognitive state where one is completely immersed in an activity". It involves intense focus, creative engagement, and the loss of awareness of time and self." What are you doing when you are in this state? DO more of that!

KEY 95

Don't focus on pushing your problems away; focus on attracting solutions.

If you can celebrate everything that comes your way, you will open yourself to a realm of pleasurable opportunities that thing has available for you.

KEY 96

What do you believe you can have?

There is an ocean of abundance. Do you approach it with a bucket or an eye drop syringe? Now is a great time to write down and affirm what you believe you can have.

KEY 97

Take your energy off what you can demand from the world and place it on what you can offer the world.

You will change the dynamic of the relationship and will find the world demanding less of you and offering more to you. Every time I've gone into a situation looking at what I have for it and not what it has for me, I got much more out of it than I would have even known to ask for. Sometimes even your requests are limitations rooted in a mindset that has been tormented by lack.

KEY 98

Move in your power or not at all

Power isn't one's ability to be dominant; power is one's ability to remain effective. Power is one's ability to define phenomena and make it behave in a desired manner. Many lack power because they give it away and choose to identify with a less authentic version of themselves.

KEY 99

5 rules to get ahead in all areas of life

1. Honor the struggle. You must see improving your life as a joyous game and maintain a positive state of mind. Understand sometimes that it's going to be frustrating and challenging. Those who avoid struggle and challenge never live the life or leave the legacy they wanted.

2. Judge after its completed not contemplation

3. No short-term thinking

4. Don't do anything for parasitic reasons

5. Stop interpreting and start observing

KEY 100

Begin and end each day with gratitude.

Always incorporate acknowledgment and thanksgiving in all you do. Be thankful for what you already have and see the miracles that come your way. This is a powerful way to attract abundance to you.

KEY 101

Step into your overflow

Challenge yourself to produce. Produce more ideas than you need for yourself so you can share and give your ideas away. That is called fruitfulness and abundance—it means working on producing more than you need for yourself so you can begin blessing others, blessing your nation, and blessing your enterprise. Abundance starts to come once someone becomes incredibly productive, moving from a flow to an overflow.

KEY 102

Dream it

Everything begins in the heart and mind. Every great achievement began in the mind of one person. They dared to dream, to believe that it was possible. Take some time to allow yourself to ask, What if? Think big. Don't let negative thinking discourage you.

You want to be a "dreamer." Dream of the possibilities for yourself, your family, and others. If you had a dream that you let grow cold, re-ignite the dream! Fan the flames. Life is too short to let it go.

KEY 103

Construct an empowering reality.

You're creating your reality right now. But chances are you're not being very intentional about the reality that you're creating. Reality is subjective; if you realize that it's a construct, if you realize that you are choosing to believe something, then you can choose to believe that you can do something about it.

Write down the beliefs that you have about yourself. On one side, list the things that empower you and move you forward. The things that make you more confident give you the courage and the audacity to move forward. On the other side, list the things that demotivate or demean you and move you away from your goals.

You can choose to believe things that empower you, and you can choose to ignore the things that move you backward. It's all a construct.

KEY 104

Stop making excuses.

Eliminating excuses is important because your future is important. If you only get the future that you work for, then what you work on is pretty important, right? Your decisions lead to your destiny. Do you believe that? You should. It's true. Sooner or later, what you do—and who you really are—determines what you ultimately achieve.

KEY 105

Realize your potential.

Think for a moment about the people you respect. Why do you admire them? You are probably drawn to them because they are full of realized potential. When we see people exerting this kind of energy, it compels us to draw ourselves closer to them and become a part of what they are doing

The wonderful thing about potential is that it can build upon itself. If you can just get the snowball rolling, the energy of motion will take over.

KEY 106

Attract opportunity.

If you can develop your skills, keep refining all the parts of your character and yourself, your health, and your relationships to become an attractive person, you will attract opportunities. Opportunity will probably seek you out. Opportunities and success are not something you go after necessarily but something you attract by becoming an attractive person.

KEY 107

Add value to others.

When you stand on the beach and watch the waves hit the shore, do you think there's any end to the water? There is, of course, but we can't comprehend it, so we think seawater is endlessly abundant. You would never deny a bucketful to a child building a sandcastle because you can refill that bucket again and again. That's how the abundance mindset works. You give away praise, recognition, ideas, knowledge, and money because you know there's plenty to go around. What you give away will come back to you a thousand times over.

KEY 108

Make the most of the infinite possibilities ahead of you.

Explore the unique, endless possibilities within you. Remember that when you work on improving yourself, you're adding to the youth, vitality, and beauty of your mind.

KEY 109

Have a hero or great person to be like.

Find a role model or great achiever to learn from. Success leaves clues. Study the greats. Gain wisdom from their mistakes. Boast knowledge from the insight they reveal.

KEY 110

Become a problem avoider.

Don't be a problem solver your whole life. At some point, you must get in the habit of avoiding problems. Become a person who is thinking and feeling good things and staying close to what aligns and flows effortlessly.

KEY 111

Repeat these affirmations

Today is a great day, and I will be great in it.

I embrace this new day and find joy in its arrival

Today I embrace the rhythm of life and let it unfold.

I focus on action to create the life I want.

On this great day, I know and trust my intuition to take me in the right direction.

This day is full of greatness and great things.

There is greatness waiting for me today.

Today I am overjoyed. Today peace is with me. Today is a great day.

This is a new day. A new opportunity. A new beginning. A great opening of wonder. A gateway of infinite possibilities.

I will find much purpose and fulfillment on this day.

This day will bring me opportunities to expand my knowledge, my understanding, my strength, & my ability.

I am great. I feel great. I am thinking great thoughts about myself and my life.

I am showing up as the greatest version of me today!

Today, I will rise to the opportunity to be greater than I have ever been.

Today, on this great day, I will be great in it.

THE GREATER EXISTENCE

Made in the USA
Columbia, SC
09 January 2025